4734
39
4.45

**AR Level:** 4.1 **Pts:** 0.5
**Quiz #:** 62167

# JIM THORPE

## DISCOVER THE LIFE OF AN AMERICAN LEGEND

Don McLeese

Rourke

Publishing LLC

Vero Beach, Florida 32964

www.rourkepublishing.com

PHOTO CREDITS: All photos Library of Congress

Cover: *Jim Thorpe in uniform*

Editor: Frank Sloan

Cover design by Nicola Stratford

**Library of Congress Cataloging-in-Publication Data**

McLeese, Don.
  Jim Thorpe / Don McLeese.
    p. cm. — (Discover the life of an American legend)
Summary: Briefly describes the life of famous American Indian Jim
Thorpe, from his early years on a reservation in Oklahoma, through his
school days in Pennsylvania, to his success at the 1912 Olympics and his
professional baseball career.
Includes bibliographical references and index.
  ISBN 1-58952-305-9
  1. Thorpe, Jim, 1887-1953—Juvenile literature. 2.  Athletes—United
States—Biography—Juvenile literature. [1. Thorpe, Jim 1887-1953. 2.
Athletes. 3. Indians of North America--Biography.]  I. Title. II.
American legends (Vero Beach, Fla.)
  GV697.T5 .M35 2000
  796'.092—dc21

2002004098

Printed in the USA

w/w

# TABLE OF CONTENTS

# A STAR IN EVERY SPORT

No **athlete** ever played more sports better than Jim Thorpe. He wasn't just a baseball star, or a football star, or an **Olympic** track and field star. He was great at every sport he tried! During the early part of the 20th century, he was the most famous athlete in America.

# BORN ON THE RESERVATION

Jim and his twin brother Claude were born May 28, 1888. They lived in a one-room log cabin on an Indian **reservation** in Oklahoma. The family was part of the **Sac** (or Sauk) and Fox **tribe** of **Native Americans**. These people were known as American Indians at the time. When Jim became famous, it made Native Americans very proud.

*A log cabin like the one where Jim Thorpe was born*

# MOTHER AND FATHER

Jim's mother, Charlotte View Thorpe, was from the **Potawatomi** tribe. Jim's father, Hiram Thorpe, was a member of the Sac and Fox tribe. Hiram's great-grandfather was Black Hawk, who was one of the bravest Native American chiefs. Jim wanted to learn all about Black Hawk as he grew older.

*The great chief Black Hawk was Jim's relative.*

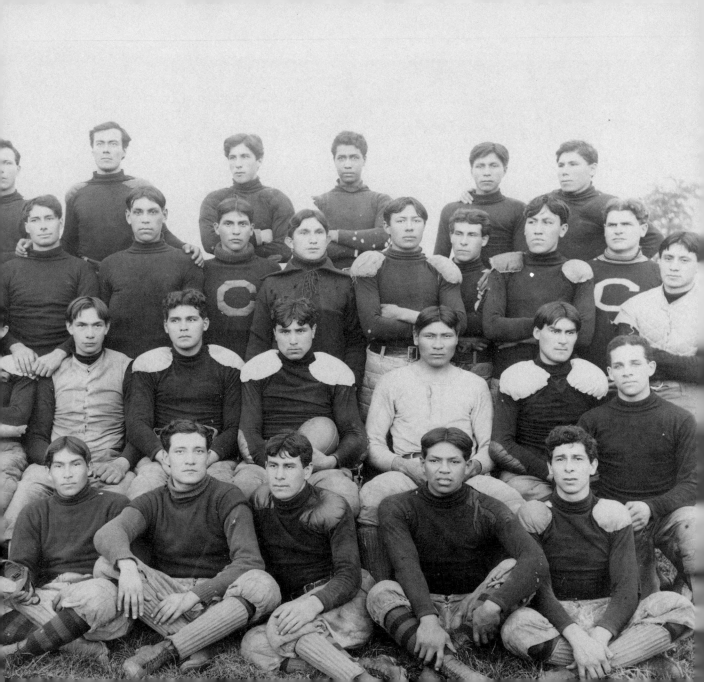

# SCHOOL SPORTS

When Jim first went to school in Oklahoma, he didn't like it. They didn't have any sports there. In 1904, Jim went to **Carlisle** Indian Industrial School in Pennsylvania. The school had students from different Native American tribes from all over the country. They also had all sorts of sports, and Jim loved them all.

*Jim played football for Carlisle.*

# POP WARNER

At Carlisle, Glenn "Pop" Warner became Jim's coach. He saw what a good jumper Jim was in track. Warner asked Jim to join the school's football team. Jim became a football star, a great runner and kicker. Pop Warner told Jim he'd help him train for the Olympics. Pop became a famous coach.

# OLYMPIC CHAMP

The Olympic Games were held in 1912 in Sweden. Jim won first place in the **pentathlon** and the **decathlon**. These events were really a number of different events, for the best runner, jumper, and thrower. When Sweden's King Gustav gave Jim his gold medals, he said Jim was "the greatest athlete in the world." Jim said, "Thanks, King."

*The Olympics made Jim a national hero.*

# LOSING THE MEDALS

Before the Olympics, Jim had once been paid a small amount of money to play baseball. The Olympics at that time didn't allow this. Jim didn't know he was breaking a rule, but the Olympics took away his medals. Other athletes said that Jim was the best and should be given his medals back. Many years later, the Olympics agreed and changed the rules.

*Jim shows kids a stance he used in the Olympics.*

A CLOSE PLAY AT SECOND

# BASEBALL AND FOOTBALL

In 1913, Jim became a major-league baseball player. He was an outfielder for the New York Giants. He was even better at football. In 1916, he led the Canton Bulldogs to a championship. He could run and tackle and kick. He once kicked a football 95 yards (86.8 meters) for a field goal!

# FAMOUS FOREVER

Jim died on March 28, 1953. After his death, a town in Pennsylvania near his school at Carlisle was named Jim Thorpe.

*Jim is in the Football Hall of Fame.*

Jim Thorpe was named to the Professional Football Hall of Fame and the National Track and Field Hall of Fame. In 1982, the Olympics gave Jim's gold medals back to his family.

# GLOSSARY

**athlete** (ATH leet) — a person who plays sports.

**Carlisle** (CAR lyl) Indian Industrial School — a school in Pennsylvania for Native Americans.

**decathlon** (dee CATH lon) — a sporting contest made up of ten track and field events.

**Native Americans** (NAY tihv uh MARE ih cunz) — the first people to live in America, called "Indians" by the Europeans who sailed to America.

**Olympic** (oh LIHM pick) games — sports competition for the world's best athletes.

**pentathlon** (pen TATH lon) — a sporting contest made up of five track and field events.

**Potawatomi** (pot uh WAT uh me) — a Native American tribe.

**reservation** (rez uhr VAY shun) — land set aside for Native Americans.

**Sac** (SACK) and Fox — a Native American tribe.

**tribe** (TRYB) — a group of Native Americans who have the same ancestors, customs, and beliefs.

# INDEX

## Further Reading

Farrell, Edward. *Young Jim Thorpe: All American Athlete*. Troll Communications, 1997.

Lipsyte, Robert. *Jim Thorpe: 20th Century Jock*. HarperCollins, 1995.

Updyke, Rosemary Kissinger. *Jim Thorpe, the Legend Remembered*. Pelican Publishing Company, 1997.

## Websites To Visit

http://www.alphacdc.com/necona/jimthorp.html

http://www.acun.com/dentons/thorpe.htm

## About The Author

Don McLeese is an award-winning journalist whose work has appeared in many newspapers and magazines. He is a frequent contributor to the World Book Encyclopedia. He and his wife, Maria, have two daughters and live in West Des Moines, Iowa.